Shoot for the Moon

by Patti Brotherton

ISBN 978-0-9824870-0-6
Copyright 2009 by Patti Brotherton

For more information, visit
www.SummerlandPublishing.com.

Printed in the U. S. A.
Library of Congress #2009940629

"No one can really pull you up very
high
—you lose your grip on the rope.
But on your own two
feet you can climb mountains."

Louis Brandeis

This book is dedicated to the agents in my
Santa Barbara offices who gave me a beautiful sculpture which reads "Always shoot
for the moon and even if you miss you will
land among the stars." It's in my back yard
and I have looked at it each morning and
felt truly inspired to write this book.
Thank you from the bottom of my heart.

Patti

Table of Contents

Foreword

Successful individuals including world class athletes and top business leaders have a common trait preparation. In today's competitive environment, preparation including goal setting, should be a common practice. Goal setting is preparation and accountability towards working a roadmap to success in all aspects of your life.

I set goals for myself at the end of each year. This includes family, business and personal goals. I then choose to prioritize these. In my personal life I put my faith in God first, then I focus on my family, which includes a 28 year marriage to my wife Sue and our four children. Then I concentrate on my business career, and aspirations. I review all of these on a regular basis and make changes whenever necessary. I follow the baseball adage "It is not if you're going to get a curveball because you will, it is what you do with the curveball when it comes." Preparation includes flexibility; your goals may change depending on the circumstances.

I believe anything is possible if you're positive and believe you can achieve it. Why do underdogs regularly win? They win because they believe they can! I just experienced this with my thirteen-year-old son and his teammates at a Lacrosse Tournament in Vail, Colorado. Over a four-day competition, sixteen teams from across the US competed. After the first day my son's team, an all-star group who had never played together before, was 1-2, but did not appear to be one of the elite teams. Then seemingly out of the running, things changed. The kids really believed in themselves. Over the next three days they won every game including the championship! They achieved this because they believed they could, even though most (including their parents) didn't think it was possible.

Every day you get to make a decision when you wake up, are you going to have a good day or a great day? You've heard the saying "Attitude is everything." It's true. Positive individuals tend to be more productive and get more out of life. If you stay positive and expect the challenges then you can "shoot for the moon" and accomplish more than you think is possible.

Patti Brotherton, author of *"Shoot for the*

Moon", has risen to the top of her profession by setting out to do so with an established goal and desire to achieve it. She has led her residential real estate offices to Number One status nationally not once, but twice with different companies. She has met personal challenges head-on and persevered because she believed that she would. Patti is a remarkable person and someone we all can admire and learn from.

Jon Cook, President and CEO
Prudential California Realty

*"All of us do not have equal talent,
but all of us should have an
equal opportunity to
develop those talents."*

-John F. Kennedy

What is Goal Setting?

CHAPTER ONE

goal , n. 1. the result or achievement toward which effort is directed; aim; end

A goal is anything you wish to have, to accomplish, to become, to see, to purchase, to enjoy, a means to help others, or something that has meaning just to you and gives you joy.

Goals can be as simple as your grocery list and as complicated as starting a new business. All goals have value in that you are accomplishing something positive.

There is no magic to setting a goal; all of us do it every day. We get to work on time. We plan a party. We go to the gym. We pick up something to eat. The real test of goal setting is when you think beyond the everyday to something you have wanted for some time, but never thought of how, or what steps it would take, to get it—for example, a new exciting job or career or a trip to Paris, France maybe.

When you start thinking right now of something you wish to have or do, set your expectations high because you <u>will</u> live up to them. You don't have to attain something this minute…you need to "shoot for it." It takes time for something important in your life. If it's too easy, you won't be   really satisfied within yourself with the accomplishment because you would have done it anyway. An example would be staying in a boring job for 15 years and making more money now than when you started. That was inevitable. How about striving to be the supervisor with much more responsibility and making the job interesting for those who work for you? That's raising your expectations.

It's important to set *reachable* goals when you are starting out, yet still set expectations high. There are many goals on the way to something big. Okay, for   example, let's talk about becoming a millionaire. That's doable, but overnight? No. You have to set goals along the way to the big goal. So, having reachable goals such as putting $10,000 away this year for a

down   payment on a rental property is doable—
you will eat out less, not purchase any new
large items for the house, not purchase some
new clothes, put off buying a new car, etc.
You get the point. If you want to become a
millionaire you need to plan on how to get there
with reachable goals. Owning property to me
was the easiest way since I know real estate and
not the stock market. You can plan your own
journey with a large goal and *reachable* goals
along the way.

Respect yourself. You deserve goals that are
worthy of the human being you are. Each of
us has the potential to be anything we want, so
don't limit yourself by not understanding how
unique you are. You can accomplish anything
you set your mind to; just write it down, believe
it, and do it.

*"All glory comes from
daring to begin."*

-Eugene F. Ware

Why Do It?

CHAPTER TWO

Why set goals? I have been urged by so many friends to write about how I have set goals over the years   because they are amazed—their words, not mine—by all that I am able to accomplish.

We have all heard friends and acquaintances say, "Some day I am going to do…" and that day never seems to come. Your *some day* is NOW because you are reading a book about goal setting so you already have the desire to do more in your life. Setting a goal is as simple as deciding on something that you wish to have or accomplish, writing it down and getting it or doing it—one step at a time.

Why do it? When you have a direction, you get where you want to go. Let me remind you of *Alice in Wonderland*. Alice came to a fork in the road and the Cheshire cat was there.

"Which road should I take?", Alice asked. The cat asked in turn, "Where are you going?" "I don't know," replied Alice. "Then it doesn't matter." So, if you don't know where you are going, it doesn't matter which way you go.

We all do better in life with something to strive for. Let me tell you how I started the goal setting adventure that I am still on. When I was eleven years old, my sixth grade teacher asked me if I wanted to participate in the student speech contest. Obviously she knew that I loved to talk and was a bit of a ham. I thought it would be fun and I applied through her to give a speech on *What America Means to Me*. My mom was excited for me and knew that our neighbor was active in the   Toastmasters group and could give me some pointers. Our neighbor helped me understand it wasn't just standing up and talking in front of people, but making sure your message got to the audience. I worked hard for that contest and wrote down on a piece of paper:

"I'M GOING TO WIN THE
SPEECH CONTEST"

That was my first written goal. I came in third place out of 200 students in my school district. I was thrilled and believed I had won. From that time on I started writing down things I really wanted and my goal setting was born. I have read many books about goal setting and gotten lots of ideas on how to reach even higher goals, but I still think the beginning of my goal setting in elementary school was what started me on the success path that I have taken over the years.

I'm a fortunate person in that I see everything from a positive standpoint and always have. It's a perspective that can be taught, but to me it came naturally. I was born enthusiastic and positive. Was my life perfect? Far from it!

My parents divorced when I was twelve years old and my mother had a nervous breakdown from it. My older brothers stayed away from the house most of time so I was left to be mom's cheerleader. My "princess" life changed when that divorce happened. I had to earn money for anything I wanted, and I did. I ironed clothes for people, cleaned houses and babysat until I reached age 16; then I started working as a typist after school for a company and loved working in an office rather than in peoples homes.

I thought it was all good because I was earning my own way at an early age; I loved it! Most importantly, from age twelve I started putting the money in envelopes by categories, movie, snacks, clothes, etc. If I really wanted something, I wrote it down and worked for it. More goals set.

Needless to say, after the divorce there was very little money in the house when I was growing up. My mom taught me many things in those years, but one that stuck and made being *poor* somewhat fun was the grocery shopping list. She would write her list and a price next to each item. She told me that if I beat the price with coupons or specials at the store, then I could have a treat. Of course, that meant a candy bar to me.

So, my goal each week was to beat her price list. I was successful almost every week—now I am not sure whether my mom made the prices higher so I could beat them or not, but she taught me that saving money on items was fun and rewarding. By the way, the amount budgeted for groceries was a whopping $5 a week!

I could go on and on about things from my youth that describe how I acquired the goal setting ways that continue to this day. I wanted to demonstrate that although my habits were formed early, it is never too late to do the same thing.

"You can't build a reputation on what you're going to do."

-Henry Ford

Before You Start

CHAPTER THREE

Something to think about…don't spend a lot of time on something negative when you can spend time on the positive.

I believe with my entire being that you must always be open to possibilities. Most people stay on the same road going somewhere although they're not sure where and never make any turns or see the incredible sights that wait right around the next corner.

Okay, is that too "out there" for you? What I mean in plain English is that opportunities are presented to all of us all the time and yet we ignore them or are afraid to take advantage of them. It almost always requires that we will have to change directions and most of us are the most comfortable doing the same thing over and over. Part of goal setting is looking at these opportunities or possibilities as positive and deciding which one is something that is a little

15

scary but truly worth trying. I don't think you need to jump to a new job every year, but look at your job differently and expand it; add something to the responsibility of your job that presented itself to you during the year. I am also not talking about changing your marriage partner; but why not change your environment with a new home or new location if your marriage seems boring (and that happens to the best of us)?

I can say this as I have been happily married to a fabulous man for more than 40 years and there were years that we did need to make changes so our marriage wasn't just existing, but thriving. All of that said, the point is you need to *see* the possibilities in a positive light when they are presented to you. This takes a little practice and once you get the hang of it you will find that your life is enhanced by all that you can do. If you find yourself being negative when a possibility presents itself, stop your thinking. Take a deep breath and put the possibility in positive terms.

Here is an example of something that happened to me. I was told by my firm that I wasn't

doing a good job and I needed to change my way of handling my office or I would be terminated. It was the first time in my career this had ever happened to me and it was devastating. I went home and for three days I thought nothing but negative thoughts about my supervisor who put me on probation, cried a lot, thought about quitting, and most of all hating the company for doing this to me.   Then I stopped, took a deep breath and thought, okay what can I do to make this right and not let it affect the people who work for me—65 people at the time. For a week I decided to incorporate all that my supervisor had suggested and see what the results were in the office; needless to say, my staff came to me and said we want the old Patti back and questioned what I was doing. So I had a meeting with the entire staff and we pledged to have the best sales record in the country and show the company that we were up to the job. We did it. What I learned was that it wasn't about me, but about the way the office was performing—I wasn't *pushing* hard enough in a positive way. When I did what they wanted and put my own spin on it, we accomplished a great deal. So, I learned from that situation that anything can be positive if you put it in the right frame of reference and learn from the

experience. I am happy to report, I have never had that happen again.

Part of goal setting is truly wanting to accomplish something; or do better in whatever career or relationship environment you are following. You can say you want something, but you have to completely embrace it to make it effective. If you are satisfied with what you have in life, then goal setting might be just an exercise. But, if you want to do more—help people, take your entire family (grandchildren, too) on a fabulous trip, write a book, start a new career, redecorate your home, create a new invention that will help humanity, or just put more funds in the bank, then you have it in you to set goals and achieve any dream. Goal setting isn't just about making money or advancing your career, it's about broadening your horizons and benefiting from every aspect of your life.

"Congealed thinking is the forerunner of failure...make sure you are always receptive to new ideas."

- George Crane

Write it Down

CHAPTER FOUR

The majority of people I know do not have written goals. That is something I don't understand as I wrote my first goal when I was eleven years old. People believe that writing down goals is silly. Why? Every company has budgets and projections on what the company is going to do *and they are written*. Is that silly? I think the opposite; once it is written I can look at it and remember what I am shooting for. Writing something on paper that you look at or put in your Blackberry makes it more of a commitment. You are committed to accomplishing your goals.

I am trying to lose some weight, so I joined a local Weight Watchers group. I am faithful in writing down what I expect to lose each week in my "tracker" and every day what I consume in food. I noticed not too many did that in my group. So, I asked the leader to do an experiment with me and I offered a gift certificate for Nordstrom's to everyone who kept their tracker for a month and recorded how much weight they wanted to lose. We held a drawing with each person's name in the drawing. We had a very successful month as a group and I believe it's because of writing down our goals and what we did each day to accomplish those goals. Of course the Nordstrom's reward sure did help.

I recall having a conversation with a gentleman who shared his goals with me and they were so different from his personality that I had to ask him if he really wanted those goals. He told me, "No, but that is what I thought I should do to be successful." Interesting. Do you think he could accomplish any of those goals? He didn't. He wasn't committed to doing something that he wanted in life, just what he thought others would think is great. He wrote them down, but he didn't *own* them. What a waste of energy that was for him. I know him today and he still has not accomplished any major goals and is, in fact, a bit lost. This is tragic to me since he has the potential to be or do anything in life. He has to truly want something for himself and work for it; not just want it because he thinks that is what others want.

Bill Cosby said it best, "I don't know the key to success, but the key to failure is trying to please everybody."

You take *steps* toward your goals, *not leaps*, and you can accomplish anything. Step One…write it down.

When you make a "to-do" list, you are goal setting. Many of us make lists each day for errands that need to be run. This is goal setting. Many make a list of groceries to pick up before going to the market. This is also goal setting. It's not a big jump to think bigger and set up daily goals. It's really fun to wake up in the morning and have your list ready; you know what you are going to do that day and it's exciting and fun. Then at the end of the day when you look at your list and all you have done, it gives you a real sense of accomplishment. That's the same with annual goals such as putting in a patio, re-landscaping the front yard, or getting a promotion at work because of all the extra effort you put in. You look at what you did on your list at the end of the year and again you feel a tremendous sense of accomplishment and that there is nothing you cannot do. That's what writing down goals does for you.

Did you know that writing down lists is contagious? I had to smile the other day when I was at my friend's house and saw her grocery list. Her children had added some things to it. A story I would like to share is about when our sons were teenagers and each worked at a grocery store bagging groceries. We always had a list going in the kitchen and if the boys needed or wanted something (school supplies, special treat) they would write it down on our list. What was a funny memory was they would also write next to the item which aisle in the store I could find the item on. I know our two adult sons now have lists on what to get for their homes, so it is contagious and becomes a habit from an early age when you share it with your family. My husband makes lists now of what he wants to do daily, but never made a list before we were married. So, again, I say making lists is contagious.

23

Your written goals are not the only ones you will achieve each year. You have hundreds of things that you do every day that are small goals. Your large goals are the icing on the cake for the year. You will have even more as you get use to writing down things.

Our sons and I wrote out a list of all the things we wanted to do each summer—Disneyland, taking the boat out, visit the water slide park, picnics, movies to see, park adventures, etc. We would check them off as we did them. It was a great way to anticipate the summer and also make sure that we got a lot of fun in. But there were also many activities that were not written down and we did those too. Writing down goals just makes it possible to do more than you had planned because it is a commitment.

"The most pathetic person in the world is someone who has sight but no vision."

-Helen Keller

Accountability

CHAPTER FIVE

Sharing a written goal with your family, your office, or a special friend definitely helps you as well. I would go away for a weekend and work on my goals by myself and then sit down with my husband and two sons and go over what I have written down and ask for their help in accomplishing the goals. They always did and were excited about what we were going to do as a family.

Again, my written goals were something I truly wanted to happen and not just something I thought I should write down for my family's sake. I didn't do it because I thought that was what everyone expected of me I did it because it is what I expected of myself and sharing it made it an even bigger commitment.

Just to make it clear, wishes are not goals. However, a personal vision definitely is. Goals are something you want to do and will do anything to see that it happens. Let me give you another example from when I was in the sales field. It was challenging since you really don't get paid anything unless you make a sale. I would spend the extra hours it took to make sure my clients understood what they were buying and the process it took even if it meant being late for a birthday party. I would follow-up on every aspect of the sale to make sure that any problems were handled even though that wasn't necessarily part of the job and I would always see the clients with some token of thanks for purchasing with me when they received the product. All of this took extra effort and time, but was critical to attaining my goals in any given year. Are you willing to do whatever it takes to achieve your vision? If yes, it's a goal. If you have a vision, you can see your goal. If not, it's not a goal.

Another example would be if your doctor tells you that you have cancer and must do a certain regimen to get well. That would be a goal, to do just what the doctor ordered and get well as quickly as possible. Would you do whatever it takes to get well? Of course! Would you share with others what the doctor expects of you?

Probably because it keeps you accountable and you have their help and support.

It is very motivating to sit down with a loved one or a fellow worker and share a goal that you have. Now they know what you are striving for and they will do all they can to help you achieve it. You don't have to spend time during the year talking about your shared goal because it will always be there between you; it strengthens the relationship. Showing someone a written goal makes it so much more real and a definite commitment.

You can make the sharing fun by including the person or persons you shared with in a reward. For example, when my office accomplished the goal I had set for the number of sales in a given month, I took everyone to lunch at a favorite restaurant. I would hire the entire place to say thank you for helping me achieve my goal. Anyone I shared a goal with also got to enjoy a reward with me when the goal was accomplished. It made it so much more fun to be accountable when you knew that you would be sharing the reward also. Use your imagination and you can come up with lots of fun rewards for goals—weekend getaways, spa treatments, fishing trips, special dinners, a movie, shopping spree, etc. See how much fun it can be?

The other special part about sharing your goals is the praise you get from your loved ones for accomplishing them. "Job well done" never gets old.

"If a man knows not what harbor he seeks, any wind is the right wind."

-Seneca

Keep it Simple

CHAPTER SIX

I need to make something else very clear: *Keep it simple*! People tend to get so elaborate in their goals they get overwhelmed. That happened to me when I had so many goals in one year I was confused about which one to actually work on first. It had a debilitating affect and took me several weeks before I revised my goals and simplified the process and started on the right path to achievement.

I believe that clear, concise goals will be much easier to follow and chart; such as, I will go to Tuscany, Italy in June with my family. It's very clear on what is to be accomplished. Of course, then I had to figure out how much it would cost, how many sales I had to make, and if I could take time off in June, to make it happen. But again, if you really want something, you will do whatever it takes.

It is my practice now to make sure I have at

31

least **four** *written goals* for three categories of my life—*family, business, and personal.* That's *four* goals for each, not 10 or more. And to make sure that I keep it simple, all my goals are written down on *one* piece of paper that I carry in my wallet. I refer to it from time to time during the year to see that I am on track with the goals and to check off those I have already achieved. It's such a concise, simple list that's easy to read and so I know just where I am going. I see people with elaborate page after page of goals; the sheer volume of that scares me. I'm a simple gal who feels less is more.

Be specific in what you are going to accomplish, but brief. No more than *four* goals for each category of your life. One category may have more goals one year than another depending on what is happening in your life.

Another example in my life was from my second full year in real estate sales (1978). I only had three goals for that year: 1)become a millionaire by the time I was 40 years old (I was 32 at the time); 2)purchase a rental property; and 3)make 100 sales. I had two sons at the time, ages 4 and 6, and in March of 1978 my husband had a bad car accident and spent almost 3 months in the hospital. I visited him every day and had help with my boys from my parents. What a year!

My husband was released from the hospital in a wheelchair and had extensive rehabilitation therapy for the next nine months. We purchased a rental property, and, most importantly, established our financial foundation for our future with the 65 sales I had. I became a millionaire by the time I was 35. Goals that were written, succinct and achievable even with the odds against me helped steer me that year. The point of establishing goals is to help you focus on specific areas that are important to you even when you are thrown curve balls and have to make immediate changes in your life to accommodate them. I didn't reach two goals that year, but definitely had a terrific year.

"As a rule...he (or she) who has the most information will have the greatest success in life"

-Disraeli

Getting Knowledge

CHAPTER SEVEN

In order to set good, achievable goals you need knowledge. What is it that you really want? A rental property? Do you know what it takes to answer phone calls from tenants with problems? Do you know what you will do if you have a vacancy? Do you have enough money in the bank to handle repairs and loss of rent? Are you mentally capable of dealing with tenants? If you know the answers to these questions or are not afraid to learn what you need to know, then you have the knowledge necessary to set the proper goal of owning a rental property.

How about losing weight? Do you know what your weight should be for your age? Do you know how many calories are in certain foods? Do you know that you have to increase your exercise routine and are you physically capable of doing that? Again, if you have the answers to these questions, you are equipped to set a good goal in this area.

How about visiting a certain country for a family vacation? Do you know the cost? How long it will take to get there? Do you need a Visa to travel there? How are you going to get around? Do you have enough knowledge of the language to feel safe? If you know the answers to these questions, you will be able to set a good goal for this.

Knowing where the majority of your business came from in the previous year is exceedingly important in setting goals for the current year. You shouldn't do things that did not produce results, but spend more money and time on what gave you the best outcome. It's always fascinating to me how many people spend time on things that really did not improve their business. Why? You need to track where your sales and business is coming from so you can project where you are going. It's really that simple.

The point is, with knowledge you make good choices and can set exceptional goals.

*"There is no security
on this earth -
only opportunity."*

-Anonymous

Motivation

CHAPTER EIGHT

It has been my experience that people who were motivated to do something in life thought of it as a goal. It may not have been formally stated that way, but nevertheless, they did have a goal. A good example of this is a friend whose daughter was getting married and she wanted to lose 25 pounds before the ceremony so she could look her best for her daughter and family. It wasn't written down, but she definitely had a goal and she achieved it. By the way, she looked fabulous in those wedding photos. The reason I write this is that *all* of us have had goals in life that we accomplished whether we stated them as goals or not. My point is that if you think about things you want and formally set those down in writing, they will become goals you can accomplish. Having one goal a year is fine, but we can all do more and you will when you formally sit down to think about what it is you really want.

We all need rewards. They can be big or small but they all have the same effect of making us feel good about something we accomplished. We have already discussed rewards with people we shared our goals with, but what about *you*? You need to think about what your reward will be when you are half way to your goal. Make it fun and something you ordinarily don't do or have. It keeps us all going in the right direction, toward our goals, when we acknowledge how far we have already come. I like trying new boutique stores, new restaurants, a limited edition book, flying to a city 3 hours away instead of driving; you get the picture. These are things I would not even think of were not for my goals.

Being motivated to take the first step is the hardest. So, make a small goal and make sure you give yourself a reward. Remember when I was eleven and wrote my first goal of winning the speech contest? My reward was a banana split. I think I have had only three of those in my lifetime and that was my first one. I can remember it as if it were yesterday.

Motivation comes in many forms. The greatest

to me is having my written goals in a place that I look at them frequently. They are where I keep my dollar bills. I guess it is a subtle reminder that my goals also help me make more money or get ahead in life and it motivates me. I know a person who put a picture of a new car on her mirror in her old car. I know of people who cut out items and put them all over their house to remind them of their goals. Whatever works for you is okay.

The key is to be reminded frequently of what you are shooting for so you stay on target. When you see your goal and you are half way there, you feel good. You can do it!

I had dinner recently with a couple who were really struggling with their business, yet it was one that should have been very successful; they are hard workers, creative, good problem solvers, and have something that is very popular right now. So, why isn't the business doing well? I believe they have not set realistic goals for this business and gone for it. They are not motivated to try new things in their business or

think "outside the box." They doubt their plans
for the future and are unmotivated to change
them. They are not going to be successful until
they sit down and set new goals, believe in
them and go for it. It's just that simple.
They need motivation to look at their business
from a different angle, and when they do new
opportunities will present themselves.

"A good business plan is money in the bank."

-Earvin 'Magic' Johnson

The Process

CHAPTER NINE

I want to improve myself so I attend lots of seminars and read tons of books. At a seminar in my second year of selling real estate I heard the speaker say that he thinks goals should be done in private and away from the pressures of everyday life. It was interesting to me that he would speak about goals since I was there to learn more about time management. I didn't buy his tapes or time management system, but I did come away from that full-day event with many great ideas I have used ever since. There were lots of gems from that particular seminar, but one that affected my life the most was to take some alone time once a year and work on your goals for the upcoming year. I started doing that the next week, taking one full day away from my work and my family to set goals for the remainder of that year. That was big for me since my husband was in the hospital at the time.

Here is the process I have been doing for over 30 years because I found it to be most successful. I take two full days away from my family all by myself out of town in a place where I can take lots of walks and just enjoy some solitude. I usually do this annually the week between Christmas and New Year's.

Okay, so the first thing is getting away by yourself without your cell phone and without checking your email. That's hard for most of us, but really essential in getting to the core of what you really want to accomplish. It doesn't have to be far away, but it definitely should be someplace where you can have peace and quiet and not be disturbed by everyday goings-on. It's best if it is in an area where people don't know you so you will not be socializing.

Secondly, you need to assess what you have done the previous year. Where are you? If you had goals, did you accomplish them? If not, why not? Did you do anything significant in your business life? Did you meet your sales goals? Why not? Is your personal life where you want it to be? Were there any family plans that got accomplished—a trip? An addition to the house? Private school? You need to sit down and look at where you have been before deciding where you are going. This is the first thing I do—write down all that I think is significant in my life from the previous year whether a goal or not. Just look at your year and think about it. It always makes me feel confident and good about my life. As I have said previously, I am very optimistic and happy so looking back always gives me a sense of fulfillment and balance. You should know that everyday I write in my "gratitude journal" five things that I am thankful for and I have for years. I take this with me when I am looking back at the year because so much is already written there and it helps me remember. There's a lot of repetition in the journal so anyone reading it can see how much I love certain things. Most important is that it is a reminder of what I did accomplish for my family or in my career during the year. This puts me in the frame of mind to do more in the coming year. But what?

Next, write down every conceivable thing that you want in life. I have pages and pages every year. Just line after line of things I would like to have, see, or do. Just let your imagination run wild. It's really fun. A little exhausting too because we tend to have self-doubts and not let our mind think we can accomplish all that we can. That's silly, but it happens to the best of us. Just start writing. Okay, another example. I would write that I wanted to: sky dive; hang glide; take the family to Australia; lose 30 pounds; earn $500,000 that year;; paint the patio; remodel a rental; plan my funeral; start stock broker accounts for the kids; take golf lessons; learn Spanish; buy a new house, and so the list goes on and on and on. I usually have hundreds of things on my lists. See how exhausting it is? It's amazing to me how the lists are different every year. The point, of course, is for you to write down things that you might have thought of doing at one time or another, but never did. Everyone is like this. We all have put off hundreds of things we thought we could do, but didn't. This is why taking the time to write this list gives you time to think about all that you might accomplish over the years. It's very illuminating.

I should tell you it was hard for me in the beginning of my goal-setting years to think of the elaborate things I come up with today. In the early years, it was simple things that motivated me—being able to get my kids in a better school or making sure my husband had all the physical therapy he could get. I never thought about skydiving in those days, or the trips to Italy. So, don't be hampered by hearing what I was striving for, let your imagination go and you will have lots to shoot for.

Now you are ready to pare your list down to four items in each of three major areas of your life: *family, business, and personal.* Imagine how hard it is going to be to take these lists and narrow them down to only four items in each. That is the challenge and why you need to be alone. You need to really search your soul and see what it is that truly "turns you on" and makes you excited about life. I think the easiest way to do this is to concentrate on one category at a time. For me, I always started with *family.* We traveled a lot as a family so that was one area I spent a lot of time on thinking we could go anywhere—what do we really want to see? Education was important for our sons, so time spent on schooling and how to pay for it was a priority. Since I have been responsible for other members of my family (namely, my parents) that would be something I always thought about—their care and what would make them happy or what it was that I had to prepare for. Family was easiest for me and so I always worked on it first because it made me so happy. I would consider the time, the cost, and how I could do whatever it is I wanted to do for or with my family.

Then I would spend time on the next category, which was *business*. I spent the most time here since what I did in this area affected the other areas of my life. I would be very specific in the goal that I wanted to accomplish including what it would take daily to accomplish it. For example, I wanted to make 25% more sales during the year by July 1. So I wrote down how many notes and calls I would make to past clients daily; how many "for sale by owners" I would see and follow-up with daily; how many expired listings I would contact daily, etc. You can see that you must be very specific and actually write down in your appointment book or put in your PDA when you were going to do the things you had planned as if it were an appointment with yourself. This would help me to plan my entire year. I knew exactly what I would be doing at 9:00 am on the Monday following my goal setting session—I was ready to go!

I would then spend time on my third category, which was *personal*. What did I want to do for myself? Read a good book monthly? Walk three times a week? Have a massage monthly? Buy a couture dress? Plan a "girls" weekend getaway? This was a hard category for me because I am satisfied with my life. I believe we do need to spend time on ourselves when we are a Type A personality and tend to go go go. The problem is that if you put off this category, it could affect your health and well being no matter what your type of personality.

Lastly, I would write down on one piece of paper the four goals I had for each of my three categories and put it in my wallet. It was such a great feeling to be so ready for the coming year.

To Recap the Process:

1. Go away by yourself, turn off your cell phone, and don't look at emails.

2. Look back at the year just completed and write down all that was done.

3. Write down every whim, every idea, every wild thing you have ever thought about doing in your life.

4. Pare your list down to four items in each of three categories—*family, business, and personal.*

5. Write your goals down.

Now you are ready to share your goals with your family, your partner, a good friend, or someone you can share with who will keep a confidence. It is not only to keep you accountable, but also to make this conversation a formal commitment with yourself by sharing it with others. This gets you and whoever you shared with excited about the year ahead. If you get any negative feedback from the individual you shared with, get another person to share with. You need positive people in your life and in your corner to shoot for the moon.

"The world stands aside to let anyone pass who knows where he is going."

-David Starr Jordan

Results

CHAPTER TEN

I have never met nor read about one person who, when totally committed to setting and achieving a goal, didn't do it. Sometimes, it took years, but it was always accomplished. One thing I do know is that when it is written down, you have a much better chance of getting ahead in this world than not. With determination and hard work, there is nothing that you cannot do in life. Benjamin Franklin said it best, "Diligence is the mother of good luck." It's hard work to go through the process of coming up with goals that you want in life, but the reward is fulfillment and success.

You can overcome huge obstacles and negative people when you set your sights on what is important to you in life. I loved the movie, *Pursuit of Happyness*, which was based on a true story of a man who was homeless and overcame many obstacles to get ahead in the stock   brokerage business in order to care for his son. Again, I say, there is nothing in life that can't be overcome. You can do it!

Results are tangible. Some of my tangible results are: I have the money in the bank that I need to enjoy my life; I have a wonderful husband and two great sons who all give me great joy; I have grandchildren that I get to spend time with and spoil rotten as often as I wish; I have friends and people in my life that make me strive to do more; I have created a monthly income for myself without having to go into work each day; I have traveled all over the world; I have beautiful homes both here in the United States as well as in Baja, Mexico; I have very little debt; I have been able to help others in not only monetary ways, but with encouragement and support; and I have had the ability to help others get better jobs and live better lives; These personal results of mine are from years of goal setting. I'm not done. What the future holds is very exciting for me and another reason I look forward to my goal setting each year. Look at your results frequently and be proud of your goal setting efforts because tangible is good.

Results can be measured. You need to write things down so you can measure what you have achieved. When you write down you want to earn $250,000 this year, you can measure that. If you do not earn that amount, think why not? Look at your results and analyze what made you miss your goal, fix any areas you can, and go again. We have already talked about accountability. Others will see your results and will mentally measure whether you were successful or not. They may not necessarily have the exact amount in every case, but they can tell if you are making more by what you are doing—a trip, more meals out, new clothes.

I have been giving you the results of my personal goal setting all throughout this book. I believe much of what I have done would not have been realized if I had not thought a great deal about the details of how to accomplish things. Many see the big picture and go for that. I want to see the big and the small along life's way. I still have much to learn and it's best learned from others. So, I spoke with several people who have their own journey and found them all fascinating. I learned something from each one of them that I am incorporating in my life today. You will be reading about these incredible people's results in the next chapter.

Remember, the reason you set goals is to get positive results!

"The only thing that stands between a man and what he wants from life is often merely the will to try it and the faith to believe that it is possible."

-Richard M. Devos

In Other's Words

CHAPTER ELEVEN

I have been very fortunate to be able to talk to remarkable people who have done extraordinary things in their lives. We all know such people, but we don't usually sit down and talk to them about their goals and how they have achieved what they have. I love sharing some of these lives with all of you. My hope is that you will derive something worthwhile for your own life by reading about these very special people.

...Find Happiness In What You Do...
Conversations with Daniel Encell

I have a great advantage over others by knowing Daniel Encell. He is a humble, incredibly successful Realtor and an overall great guy. I know personally what he has accomplished in life so I was anxious to talk with him about his goals. He feels that his goal setting came somewhat naturally as he has always had a competitive personality.

He told me his dad gave him $1 for every A on his report card in elementary school, so he couldn't wait for his report card. It was the beginning of his thinking of goals and getting rewards for attaining them. He was sent to a boarding school when he was a freshman in high school; he said it was a very competitive atmosphere so he fit in quite well. Of course it helped that his dad offered him a cow (he lived in ranching country) to get all As. Did he do it? Yes! He went on to college and then law school with the goal in mind to earn a lot of money.

In the early 1990s he was buying lots of lottery tickets and started thinking "What would I do if I won? What would I do differently in my life?" He realized that his goals were changing to define what he wanted in the quality of his life and how he wanted to spend his time. His long -term goals had rewards such as owning a beach property, owning a lake property, owning an airplane, and owning a vineyard. Did he do it? Yes!

He tells me that his first written goal was in 1995 (by the way, he dug it out of his file and read it to me) when he wrote his first business plan for his real estate. His goal was $210,750 in gross income and $57,456 in expenses, netting him $153,294 in income. As he told me, in the beginning of his career he was much more specific than he is today. He feels his goals are more generic in that he knows approximately what he wants in sales volume and gross revenues, but more importantly what he wants in the way of the quality of his life. He fine tunes his business each year in finding things he can do better such as not working weekends and still maintaining his sales numbers. His most important goals today are having a happy life, good personal fitness, quality family time, and an overall sense of accomplishing what he set out to do.

When a friend of his ran for public office and didn't do well because young professionals didn't have a support network in place, he decided to start the Santa Barbara Young Professionals Club, which still exists. This is a group that networks together helping in the community by raising lots of money and

awareness for various charitable causes. A worthwhile goal that epitomizes what Dan is all about; giving back to the community just as he gives back to his profession. He never turns down an opportunity to share his wisdom with fellow Realtors and has spoken at many professional venues including guest appearances on television shows about current real estate market conditions.

Dan feels that his major accomplishments to date are having a fabulous family, good friends, starting the Santa Barbara Young Professionals Club, having a good reputation among realtors and raising awareness of just what a realtor should be, as well as enjoying an amazing life-style.

He is not afraid of "stretching" for his business or family and will go the extra yard it takes to reach the next level. So who knows what the future holds for this very successful entrepreneur.

...Do Unto Others...
Conversations with Jim Huff

Another interview that was stimulating and fun for me was with Jim Huff because I couldn't wait to hear about his goals and his journey in becoming the successful entrepreneur he is today. He tells me that goals are critical for knowing how well you are doing. He thinks goal setting is a motivational tool. He told me that   reason he and I were talking was because he set a goal for himself; he wanted to have the finer things in life and that took having money. He told me that he got into real estate because he felt you made the most money at the point of sale and real estate was a high ticket item that he could sell. He wanted to be in control of how much he could make.

In the early 1970s he attended a seminar about goal setting and heard the speaker say that if you get one listing out of every 15 cold calls you were doing well. He finally had a number to shoot for. What did he achieve? He got one out of every three! He also watched a salesman handle the acquisition of listings as a business that had contact goals; he said to himself "I can

61

do that!" Those two things were his motivation for starting to goal set. His first written goal: 50 listings a year, which he maintained during his long career in real estate.

In 1975 he started his own company. He determined right away that he couldn't be a one -man show so he started hiring other agents to work for him. He figured out early in life it's still his motto to this day, if you treat people right they will treat you right. People want to return the goodwill they have received. He knew that having his own company was a risk, but he wasn't looking for comfort; he wanted to control his own destiny. He was definitely driven by the fear of not making it, so he just would not go home; he worked until the job got done.

He tells me that he eats, sleeps, and dreams his business and loves all of it. He will do whatever needs to be done. He has written goals and sets them with a team of people who work with him; his staff tracks everything, which makes it easier to set budgets and goals for the year.

His long-term goals were to make enough money to have nice things in life—homes, cars, vacations,   airplane, motor home, boats, all the fun toys that you could imagine. He got them all! He wanted to visit all 50 States and did it! Now he wants to go to all the continents and he's almost there. He loves meeting people in different walks of life. He tells me that he gets bored easily and he wants to see *everything*. He loves every new experience. According to Jim life is good. He has provided a secure financial position for this family and that was important to him.

He has been asked many times, "Did you ever think you would grow the company to the size it is?" He says that he always sees opportunities and takes advantage of them. His philosophy is, if it doesn't make sense, it won't work. If it makes sense, he is a hard driver and will get it done. The real estate market has gotten tough from time to time, but he adjusts and keeps the company alive; maybe he couldn't grow as fast as he wanted, but that was okay. He says, "Bad times create opportunities as well as good times," he is always open to those opportunities.

Jim told me that he got off balance for awhile with all the charitable work he did and had to make changes so he could spend more time on his business. He says that now he is selective and involved in what he enjoys and believes in more than what would help his business. For example, he provides scholarships for his alma mater as well as serves on several boards.

He feels that his greatest accomplishments to date are being the CEO of his company, having a good family and being able to spend time with his grandchildren, having the resources for fun things in life such as putting the kids on a plane and going to an amusement park; and most important being with people he loves and admires. He believes he has been abundantly rewarded in life so far.

Since there is a lot more life left to discover, the sky's the limit where Jim is concerned.

...Seeing The Big Picture...
Conversations with John Safri

Since writing this book, I have been curious

about people who I see are successful and I want to know whether they have goals or not. I would like to share a story about John Safri who owns JFS Construction. He started his business with $7,000 in a rented space of 1,600 square feet, which he furnished with Office Depot furniture, supplies and equipment to make it look like it was successful (Office Depot had a program of no payments for six months and he took advantage of that!). He said he had to fill the desks with people and that is just what he did. He told me that in the early days he never went home until all the work was done, and since he and a receptionist were the only employees, he had very long days.

His long-term goals were set in his mind many years ago: open his own company; have his home paid for; have a wife and kids; have $1Million in the bank. He has done all of this. His goals have changed as he has achieved them. He has owned his company for 10 years now, he is building a bigger home and yes, his other one is paid for. He has a wife and two children, and way over $1million in the bank. Is he satisfied? No, he wants to expand the company with more help so he can take time off to enjoy his family. He is learning and studying the stock market because he feels you need to be involved to succeed and not count on someone else to take care of your money. He owns rental properties and is maintaining a life-style of comfort yet still way within his means.

He told me that he absolutely believes in goal setting and when he looks at his company numbers he always wants to increase them by 25% - he has grown his company every year since he started it. He tells me that he is always shooting for bigger numbers than he can reach, but he usually gets to 80% of his goal each year. He always sets monthly goals for his staff and then   rewards them when they hit their goals; he believes that if he shares his goals with his staff they will work harder to help the company as well as themselves.

One thing he learned from the hard work he has put into building his company is that you need to delegate and take time for yourself and then you can accomplish even greater goals. He told me that in setting his goals he always remembers where he came from so he doesn't get "cocky" thinking it will always be there—he plans for downturns in his business and that has paid off for him. The first goal that really made an impression on him was to have $1million in sales in his company; it took him one year to do it.

He feels his greatest accomplishments are owning the company, having a great reputation, making more money than he expected, and having a wonderful wife and kids. John is a super example of someone who had setbacks in his career, but learned from the experience and turned it into something positive by starting his own company and knowing just where he was going with it.

...How High Can You Go...
Conversations with Greg Brown

I had the privilege of talking with Greg Brown, a young man in his 30's, about his success and how he has accomplished so much at a young age. Greg told me that goal setting is a big part of his business life and matters greatly to him— he knows where he is going and has time lines to get there. He thinks that goal setting came naturally to him since he grew up with two brothers (both of whom are also successful) and they all had a hunger for things they never had as kids because money was tight. His parents were divorced and his mom was a school teacher, so they had to watch their pennies when they were young and all the boys worked to get those extra things that all teenagers want. Greg has an attitude of "I can," which is reflected in his daily life.

The first major goal he set for himself was in his second year of college—he wanted to get a job with one of the "Big Six" accounting firms. That was his major focus and he was going to do it. When he graduated with two degrees—one in accounting and the other in communications—he secured his first job with Anderson Consulting. First goal achieved! He also became a certified public accountant and two years later became a Senior Consultant. Another goal achieved.

Greg's first written goal was when he got into the car business as controller for a company in California. He would write down what he wanted to accomplish for the company and focused all his attention on that; he feels a good employee should make his company successful. He also had a personal goal of wanting to become the general manager of the company; he did that in 1 ½ years! He stayed long enough to accomplish all that he wanted to for the company and started to think that he needed something bigger and better to concentrate on. His mission was to purchase his own car dealership and he gave himself two years to do it. Of course, he did it!

He had other personal goals along the way like becoming a millionaire by the time he was age 30; he did it at 27! He wanted rental properties and started buying those when he was 24 years old and still in college. He bought three townhouses with 3% down on each, lived in one with roommates paying rent and rented out the other two. After the property gained in value, he sold them and used the money to buy apartment buildings, which was one of his long-term goals.

When I asked him about his greatest achievements he was very humble. First was being married to the right person and having three great kids; then having friends, and being happy with his life. In business he is proud of the goals he has achieved and records exceeded as well as having rental properties that have done well.

He had very aggressive goals set for the year 2009, but in 2008 the car industry took a deep dive into a recession. He had to swiftly change his thinking and plan how he would weather the storm and keep his business secure. He was able to reduce his expenses more than he thought possible and establish more realistic goals for the remainder of the year. This major change in the economy also made him realize that instead of always thinking how high can he go and how much more money can he make, it was time to think about enjoying the fruits of his labor. The major milestone in his life has been achieved so far—being able to live off his investments and enjoy personal things more.

Greg isn't done with goals by a long shot, but he sees that you need to take each day and make it special for yourself and family. He's a great success story!

...Hardship Turned To Bonus...
Conversations with Anthony Orefice

I interviewed a 35-year-old man who has such a great attitude about life that I needed to know if he also had goals or not. Let me give you background so that you gain perspective on this individual as you read about him. Anthony Orefice graduated from high school and was working for UPS; he was 19 and having a fun time in life as most 19 year olds would be. One evening he was drinking with a friend they both had too much to drink, but Anthony less so than his friend. Anthony decided to drive home on a friends' motorcycle that night. Anthony decided to give him a great ride and went speeding up the mountain, which is the last thing he remembers about that night. He isn't sure what happened, but was told that his friend fell off throwing the motorcycle off balance and causing him to crash into a pole, breaking his back in three places. He was on life support in the hospital for 1 ½ months and eventually came out of the experience as a paraplegic. His friend only had some scrapes and bruises. Anthony could be mad at life, but instead he found his faith.

Today he is a partner in a medical supply company, married, and has an adopted son. I asked him what was one of his first goals after getting out of the hospital and he told me to purchase a Hummer. That's quite a goal since he is in a wheelchair and has to lift himself into the car. He got it! He has used it to be an inspiration for others when he visits hospitals and shows patients that you can do anything if you have the will, work hard for it, and just do it. He encourages people on a daily basis that you can overcome anything.

I asked him how he goes about setting goals and he told me that first he prays; then does a lot of thinking; then gives thanks because he believes he has gotten more than he could ever believe he would get. He   believes that goals are necessary in life to keep going.

He has much more to accomplish and is working on a new career in real estate and wants to get a pilot's license and his own airplane, to name just two. He still does off-road racing and was able to race at Anaheim Stadium, which was a dream come true. He speaks at various venues, conducts a monthly support group at the hospital, and keeps alive by encouraging others when they are in their darkest days that things do get better. He is living proof.

Anthony doesn't write his goals down, but he has his lists and knows where he is going. He will be whatever he chooses; life is good for him because he chooses to make it that way.

...There's No Quitting...
Conversations with Mary Dan Eades

It was a delight listening to Mary Dan Eades, M.D. talk about her goal setting and all the adventures in her life to date. She definitely believes in setting goals and tells me the first goal she really thought about was when she was in junior high school and was trying out for cheerleader. The night before the try out, she pulled a hamstring—that was a big blow. She had always achieved whatever she wanted in school and this was the first time she fell short in not making the cheerleader squad. What she learned was even with hard work you might fall short so you always have to be ready to pick yourself up and go again. She made

Cheerleader the next year! Mary Dan believes you learn more from failure than you do from success.

She has written goals and she also visualizes her goals. She wakes up during the night with a goal in her head and visualizes achieving it right down to the minute details. With her books, she always has to come up with a title first, then she can go ahead and focus on the content. She and her husband make a practice of having clearly defined goals and she told me that sometimes it is hard to put goals into word. So they work on that. They use organization goals, thinking "What roles do I play in my life?" For each role they set 3 goals a week. For example, her role as grandmother, what can she do to be a better part of the grandchildren's life that week; for her role as author, what does she need to contribute to the book this week (research, writing, etc.); for her role as president of the Santa Barbara Choral Society, what does she need to do to get more people to a concert this week; and for her role as speaker, what does she need to do to prepare for the speech, and so on. She always has "time out" scheduled for her own personal time such as a walk on the beach. She feels that she keeps balance in her life through these organization goals.

Goal setting came naturally to her as part of her upbringing. Her dad was a big influence in her life as he was a very capable person and accomplished whatever he set his mind to. She said, "I grew up without a pass," meaning, if you said you would do something, you had to do it. There was no quitting because her Dad would not tolerate it. He would encourage her to be more thoughtful in what she wanted to accomplish because once you committed to it you had to do it. As she explained, when you set a goal you are giving yourself your word that you will do something. She was taught never to break your word, even to yourself.

Sometimes there are delays in obtaining your goals and you need to learn patience. It took her 10 years to get the home they wanted in Santa Fe, New Mexico. As your life changes, so do your goals. The saddest thing is not having any goals—you are adrift without them. She is refining her goals all the time.

She told me she has many proud accomplishments in life starting with paying for all three of her sons to get through college, and each have a car upon graduation. Money was tight and even though the boys were bright they did not have scholarships, so it was up to mom and dad to pay for their education. That was at a time when they were building their clinics and money was tight. They did it and are very proud of their sons and where they are taking their lives today.

Getting through medical school was another big accomplishment since she had not intended to be a doctor when she was in college; originally she was interested in math and microbiology. She changed colleges in her junior year to follow a boy, had a bad car accident and had to drop out of school for two years to pay for bills. She decided during this two year hiatus she wanted to have a more financially secure career so she went into medicine as it would combine her love of science and math with a career that would make her more money. She set goals and a timeline for getting into medical school and was accepted before she even received her final college degree. She was told that she wasn't going to make it when she went back to college and that just made her want it even more.

She and her husband are both doctors and built four clinics in Arkansas and had the largest general practice in their metro area. They sold their general practice, but kept their nutritional practice. Because they were medical entrepreneurs, they had periods of feast and famine. They worked seven days a week to keep afloat. It all paid off as they sold their practice and moved into a lucrative writing career.

Her husband, Mike, influenced her interest in writing. She tells me she just wanted to write a book and be published. She was given a topic (arthritis, which had great meaning because of her dad's arthritis) and she wrote about it and found it to be something she really enjoyed, could do fast, and was good at. She and Mike have written over 14 books and had a wonderful best seller that sent them all over the world on personal appearances.

They were travelling so much that she didn't feel she had any roots. They had homes in

several different cities, but they were home so
little during this seven year period, and because
she needed to stay put, they sold their home in
Santa Fe and bought a second home in Santa
Barbara. She wanted to get involved in the
community and since she loved to sing, the
Santa Barbara Choral Society was the answer
for her. She heard they were doing a tour of
Europe and she wanted to sing Mozart in
Vienna so she joined the group. She now serves
as president of this 100-voice ensemble. She
has settled in.

All of this said and done, she thinks the
greatest thing she has done in life is
successfully raise three great sons.

What's next? She says she is always open to
new adventures. It's a big world.

Come on Toto…
Conversations with Nancy Hogan

I couldn't write about goal setting without
thinking about my dear friend, Nancy Hogan.

She has been such a special part of what I have done in my life and we share very similar beliefs about business and family. Goal setting to Nancy Hogan is an important part of "Going down that yellow brick road" to quote her. Without a destination, she wouldn't have been able to do what she has done.

She tells me goal setting came naturally as she was one of eleven siblings, which made for an inherently competitive environment. She and her siblings are all successful in their own careers and she credits her mom for this. Her mom's favorite word was "adjust"; in other words make the best of things. Her parents always told her that honesty and hard work pay off; and in their words, "There is no right way to do the wrong thing." As a kid she always had goals and says she has an innate ability to dream thanks to her family.

Nancy's first written goal was when she was thirteen years old. She earned money teaching swimming so she could buy her mother a sewing machine to make her mother's life a little easier. She did it! Nancy wanted a 1965 blue Mustang and she cut out a picture of the car and put it up in her room. Her father told her that if she saved $500 and one year's insurance, she could buy her car. She did it! (By the way, she still has that Mustang!) Then after being married a short while, her husband changed jobs and was out of work for a time, and her goal was to make enough money to pay the mortgage payment; she painted ceramic bowls and other items and held home parties to sell them. She was able pay the mortgage every month until her husband was again employed full time. She did it and is still proud of that time!

When she is thinking about her goals, which she always writes down, she looks at where she is personally, where her family is, and where her office is. Where do we go from here? What will I be satisfied with? She believes in challenging herself and then rewarding immediately when she has reached her goals. Her biggest business goal is to always make the office profitable. Nancy is very balanced in that her personal and business goals are equally important to her. She has figured out that as she gets older she wants to spend more quality time with family, which seems to her a natural change from striving to be the best business person in the nation.

Her major goals in life were to be happy, raise a nice family, give back to others, and always have enough money to be comfortable. Of course she has done all of this.

Let me name just a few of her major accomplishments to date: She has been married 42 years, has two wonderful productive daughters, was a top selling agent for her company the entire time she was a selling agent, and was a top manager in her company for years. She was appointed by the governor to the seven member Florida Real Estate Commission and the commissioners elected her the chairman of the commission. She was appointed by the Miami/Dade County Mayor to the first Mortgage Fraud Task Force. She was the Chairman of the Realtor Association of Greater Miami and Beaches, and a District Vice President of Florida Association of Realtors.

Nancy has experienced lots of changes in the companies she has worked for. She tells me that every time the company changes with new management, she steps back and looks at her goals because she needs to have empowering people around her, and when they keep changing she doesn't know who they are. In order to stay focused on her goals she keeps looking at the people around her and knows she can make a difference in their lives; that is how she stays motivated with change.

There is so much more for Nancy to do and she can hardly wait to see where the next opportunity will come from.

"If you have built castles in the air, your work need not be lost; that is where they should be. Now put the foundations under them."

-Henry David Thoreau

Budgeting

CHAPTER TWELVE

Part of goal setting is putting a specific budget together that will support the financial challenge of achieving that goal. The budget should encompass each area of your life for one year—family, personal, and business. It's one thing to set a goal, but quite another to know how much it will cost or how much it will increase your annual financial outlay. Think about it. Having actual numbers in front of you as you start the year gives you a clear picture of what to expect.

Let me give you examples. You may have a goal to put in a new kitchen this year. How much will it cost? Let's say you have $20,000 set aside for this project. After the work has begun, you'll discover it's so much more rewarding and fun to beat your budget instead of increasing it. You don't have to spend it all or exceed the budget. I hear quite frequently about projects going over budget. Why? There are ways to save money and still have the beautiful kitchen you want. For example, do some of the work yourself. Be smart and stick to a budget because that's what will enable you to shoot for that goal. I always try to beat my budget, but if I can't, I adjust and still stay within what I have budgeted.

Another goal may be to work out at a gym three times a week. Set the amount you will spend on this activity and stick to it. If rates go up or you want to change gyms, you can negotiate with different facilities and find one that fits your budget. Again, beating your budget is fun!

Another goal may be to have a housekeeper every week to help around the house and free up time for other activities. Shop around and find someone who will do all that you want and more—perhaps the laundry? Are you going to give this person a little bonus at holiday time? Set a definite price down on paper that you want to pay for this service and then find the person who will work for this amount.

Perhaps you have the goal of learning a new skill or hobby and want to take a class at the local community college. Would this require you to purchase equipment? Do you need to have a babysitter during the time you will be away? Can you find a class some other way without the fees? Set the amount you are willing to spend and then find a way to do it.

Perhaps you have a business goal to increase your income by a certain amount. You'll need to budget how much you will invest in development and growth. Be honest and don't start pulling back or spending more; stick to your budget. An example would be the amount you budget for marketing resources in the sales field; get creative and negotiate with newspapers, magazines, or use other venues like mailers to get your message out when rates go up and you find yourself being pinched. You have a budget, it's a goal. Stick to it!

Remember the chapter on Changing Goals? Things happen in life unplanned and out of the blue. All of a sudden you don't have the money or time to achieve a goal. That's okay, that's life! You can change as well as postpone goals.

When you are reviewing your goals at the end of the year, the budget you have created also needs to be reviewed. You need to feel good about what you have accomplished including staying within your budget. Many people have told me about their goals, but have no idea of what they will cost. That's not really setting goals.

Remember, your budget is another goal!

*"The indispensible first step
to getting the things you want
out of life is this:
decide what you want."*

-Ben Stein

Discipline

CHAPTER THIRTEEN

All that you have been reading about takes discipline. Discipline is a habit. You can develop any habit by repeating the same thing for 30 days. I learned early in life that if you want something you have to get it yourself, so when I was young I was pretty disciplined about getting my work done fast so I could swim in the pool or go to a movie. My mom required everyone in the house out to do chores in order to enjoy what we had. My brothers and I were pretty good about doing our work before play (of course, if we didn't my mom could be relentless in her discipline). From this early time in my life I found that if I did my job first, I had more time to do other things I really enjoyed.

So, you can guess that I am not a procrastinator. I am very disciplined and if I have something to do that is on my daily list, it gets done. One thing I have found that works best for me is to have a written daily list because it really bugs me not to get that list done. I don't prioritize formally, but anything that will accomplish my long term-goals always gets done first. It's automatic for me. If you are new to goal setting you may have to spend some time on prioritizing so you do important things that will help you in your life first, and put off such things as straightening out your desk contents. Spending time on unimportant items that will not help you with your goals is just foolish and we all do it. Most importantly, do the things first that will get you what you want!

A book that I found really helpful in my goal setting discipline is *Power of Focus* by Jack Canfield, Mark Victor Hansen, and Les Hewitt. It's not a new book (published in 2000) but a great reference resource when you get off track. It is excellent in helping people who want to do more in life and find the power to be disciplined and focused on what it is they want. This book inspired me to keep a list of 100 things I want to do before I die, which is now a part of my goal setting process. I review that list and cross off what I did and add to it. It's always got 100 things on it. It's incredible how much you do!

The movie, "The Bucket List", was about having a list of things you want to do before you die and was also inspiring as well as very humorous. How incredible it was to see this movie and realize in looking at my list that there is not much I am missing in life because of the discipline I have had in writing goals and going for them all these years. If I were to die tomorrow, I would feel good about all that I have done in life with little in the way of regrets.

"You gain strength, courage and confidence by experience which you must stop and look fear in the face....
You must do something you think you cannot do."

- Eleanor Roosevelt

Overcoming Fear

CHAPTER FOURTEEN

We all have fear of failure. It's one thing to write down that you will knock on 50 doors today and talk to at least 30 people and quite another to actually do it. We all fear that someone will reject us. And, of course, some will. So what? I have to confess that when I was new to real estate and heard that knocking on doors was a good way to get to know people in your neighborhood, and let them know you are in the business, I was scared stiff. This is one area in which I procrastinated for six months because I was so fearful of the experience of rejection. I actually had stomachaches before I knocked on the fist door. My goal that first time was to just get through my entire area; I did it and the result was I got a listing and a sale on the last street of my area. I couldn't believe it! I was hooked! Remember the worst thing that can happen is that we are rejected, but we are not going to die from it. To

93

keep going when the door slams is what separates winners from losers. It takes some practice to keep going when you really don't want to and I have some practical exercises that help to overcome our fears:

1. Before you attempt to tackle something hard call someone who thinks you are the greatest person on earth. You don't have to talk long; but feel how good it is to know that people trust you and believe in you. Facing difficult situations can be debilitating if we think about them too much before acting. So, pick up the phone and hear someone's voice who likes you. It's easy and fast. Then act.

2. Set a small goal of calling one difficult person. When you overcome that, you are ready to overcome bigger things. Putting off dealing with people slows down your whole day. Deal with it, feel better and go on to bigger things.

3. Write an "ideal scene" as to what the results will   actually be in the present tense of whatever it is you are fearful of. Let me explain more fully.

One of my associate managers conducted a training program on creating "ideal scenes" for your business. I sat in on her session and was moved to try it. Well, needless to say, I'm still doing them. You write down a paragraph or full page of how you wish an event to take place in your life; for example…

"I am calling on XYZ Company today with enthusiasm and insight into how I can help them make huge amounts of money by purchasing my product. I am received with welcoming smiles and a genuine interest in what I have to offer. The CEO is very excited about having this product on his shelves and asks intuitive and specific questions showing his overwhelming interest in the product. I am closing the sale with gratitude that this company will be getting a fabulous product that will be lucrative for them and I have started a genuine friendly relationship that will bode well into the future."

Once I write the scene, I put it in my folder and go tackle the project. I have written hundreds of them, not only about business, but also about my friends and family. It is really fun to do once you get into it. It's always positive and, believe it or not, the outcomes generally follow your "ideal scene." It's not exact, but when you believe it you achieve it.

4. Just do it!

Fear is healthy; it means you are human. Overcoming fear is what makes each day a little bit more exciting. Remember when you learned to drive and the fear you had in the car your first solo trip? You overcame that and now it is second nature to get in the car and go.

"Dad always said you've got to stay flexible... Dad thrived on change, and no decision was ever sacred."

- Jim Walton
on his father, Sam Walton

Changing Goals

CHAPTER FIFTEEN

Okay, you have your goals written down and life throws you a curve. Change your goals. Nothing is set in   concrete. But you should only change your goals for   something that is bigger than you.   This is what I am talking about.   I had specific goals I was actively working to achieve when I received a telephone call in March of 1993 that radically changed my life.   I was told that a man who had been stalking me and my family wanted to kill me. This was a man I fired two years earlier because I felt he was mentally unbalanced. Wow! I sat back and couldn't believe what I heard. I was told that he was being incarcerated and treated for a mental disorder and they would advise me when he was being released. I was leaving for a conference in two days and here was this news. I went because I was scheduled to give a speech at the conference. I had lunch with a friend from Atlanta while I was there and he asked if I would ever leave the state of California. Good timing. Yes, I think I would since our sons were in college; why not? Well, I had four job offers from that conference. I moved to Florida 60 days later, a place I had only visited briefly and took over the management of an office there. I didn't know the laws, had to get a broker's license, relocate without anyone in California knowing where I was going, had to sell our house, and my husband had to retire from his job. Did you think my goals for the year changed? Of course! I had new exciting experiences ahead and my family was safe. I immediately sat down and wrote out new goals about the move, the boys, my husband, our rental properties—it all fell into place. To this day, we think the three years I spent in Florida were a great blessing to us.

Here's another example. In January of our third year in Florida our sons called and wanted us back in California. There wasn't a second's hesitation on our part, we would come back, but we didn't want to return to the same city we left and the boys were good with that as long as we came back. I gave 90-days notice, sold our house in Florida and we moved again across the country to a city where we knew only one person personally and I had no job. Did my goals change drastically from what I had originally planned? You bet! I can again say that the move was a blessing and one we have never regretted.

You should give your goals a hard look after six months to make sure you are on track. An example in my life using this six month check is when I took over the management of an office, and I was not hitting any of the goals I had set for it. I analyzed why and realized I had set goals for the office before I really knew what I was getting into. I was frustrated and unhappy with the results and very hard on myself. With this six month check, I realized I was approaching the office from the wrong perspective, made the changes I needed to, reset my goals and away I went. I reached the new goals I set for that year.

When life evolves, you evolve with it. It's important to be able to change your goals, but even more important to have them. When life gives you turns you hadn't expected, you turn with them and make the best of it. It's easy to just throw your goals away when something happens and not rewrite them, but then you will be missing something important in your life. You should experience fulfillment in all that life gives you, so change your goals, write them down and go for it!

"The mind is the limit. As long as the mind can envision the fact that you can do something, you can do it - as long as you really believe 100%"

- Arnold Schwarzenegger

Final Thoughts

CHAPTER SIXTEEN

I hope I have shown you that having goals is essential for not only getting ahead in your career or profession, but in your everyday life as well. The difference written down goals make is that they get accomplished while all the others are on the sideline in a "some day" category. You are ahead of the game and life is a game. Make each day fun and full of experiences so that you will never say, "Someday I'm going to…"

I leave you with this final quotation from Robert Louis Stevenson:

"To be what we are, and to become what we are capable of becoming, is the only end of life."

"First comes thought, then organization of that thought into ideas and plans; then transformation of those plans into reality. The beginning, as you will observe, is in your imagination."

Napoleon Hill

About the Author

Patti Brotherton is a nationally recognized consultant, author, and speaker. She is founder and president of PAB Performance Partners which is dedicated to helping agents, managers, and companies achieve higher levels of success.

During her thirty-four year career in real estate she was named the top sales associate in the nation for four years with a major franchise firm—averaging over 100 sales per year (and working only nine months out of the year full time). Patti has managed six different offices bringing them all to top performance in the state, both in California and Florida. The last office she managed was named Number Nine in the country regardless of size with a major franchise firm—her agents averaged $10,000,000 in sales per agent in 2007.

She has sat on the Board of Directors for the Montrose Chamber of Commerce, Optimists

Club, Los Angeles Rams Booster Club, Abused Women's Shelter, Friends of Lobero Theater, Santa Barbara Symphony, as well as serving as a leader in her church. Being involved in the community and helping others is a large part of her lifestyle.

Referenced Bibliography

Thoughts from Great Women by Patricia Martin

Zig Ziglar's little book of Big Quotes by Zig Ziglar

The Best of Success by Katherine Karvelas

Made It by Hulton Getty

Whatever It Takes by Bob Moawad with Dan Zadra

To Your Success by Dan Zadra

32 Ways to be a Champion in Business by Earvin "Magic" Johnson

Great Quotes from Great Leaders by Peggy Anderson

Quotations of John F. Kennedy by JFK

The Road to Success by Larry Wall and Kathleen Russell

Leadership 101 by John C. Maxwell

Reach for the Stars by Kerren Barbas

The Best of Success by Wynn Davis

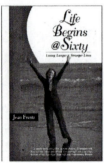